WATERGATE

WATERGATE

Deception in the White House

BY DANIEL COHEN

Spotlight on American History

THE MILLBROOK PRESS
BROOKFIELD, CONNECTICUT

Photographs courtesy of Corbis-Bettmann: pp. 9, 10, 26 (bottom),
36, 38; *The Washington Post*: p. 12; Carl Albert Center
Congressional Archives, University of Oklahoma: p. 17 (top left);
John Paul Filo: p. 22; AP/Wide World Photos: pp. 25, 26 (top); ©
1997 The New York Times Company: p. 39; Doug Marlette: p. 44;
National Archives: p.51; © 1973 Philip Lief and Marcel Feigel: p. 56.

Library of Congress Cataloging-in-Publication Data
Cohen, Daniel, 1936-
Watergate: deception in the White House / by Daniel Cohen.
p.   cm.— (Spotlight on American history)
Includes bibliographical references (p.   ) and index.
Summary: Discusses the break-in at the Watergate complex in
Washington, D.C. in 1972 and the events that unfolded thereafter,
resulting in the downfall of a president and a distrust of government.
ISBN 0-7613-0271-9 (lib. bdg.)
1. Watergate Affair, 1972-1974—Juvenile literature.
2. Nixon, Richard M. (Richard Milhous), 1913-1994—Juvenile
literature. 3. United States—Politics and government—1969-1974—
Juvenile literature. [1. Watergate Affair, 1972-1974. 2. Nixon,
Richard M. (Richard Milhous), 1913-1994.] I. Title. II. Series.
E860.C58   1998
973.924—dc21   97-26881   CIP   AC

Published by The Millbrook Press, Inc.
2 Old New Milford Road
Brookfield, Connecticut 06804

CONTENTS

THE BREAK-IN

Frank Wills, a security guard at the
office-hotel-apartment complex called
Watergate in Washington, D.C., came
to work as usual just before midnight
on Friday, June 16, 1972.

One of his first tasks was to make sure the basement doors were secure. He found that several of them had been taped so that they would stay unlocked. Wills called a superior for advice. Then he called the police. Three plainclothes policemen in an unmarked car responded.

They began a search of the office building. On the sixth floor they found the same sort of tape on the locks of the door leading to the stairwell.

The sixth floor contained the offices of the Democratic National Committee (DNC). As the police walked through the offices they saw someone crouching behind a desk in one of the cubicles. Officer John Barrett had his revolver out. He shouted, "Hold it. Come out."

Five men emerged from the cubicle. They were all dressed in business suits and they were all wearing blue rubber gloves. They offered no resistance, and said they were unarmed. Sergeant Paul Leeper recalled, "They were probably five of the easiest lockups I have ever had."

This rather undramatic arrest set in motion a chain of events that led to one of the greatest political scandals in American history, ending with the resignation of a president.

It was immediately obvious to the police that these men were not ordinary burglars. When they were taken to the police station they all gave false names at first, and refused to give addresses. Four of the five were carrying between two hundred and eight hundred dollars in new hundred-dollar bills with

The Watergate complex. The Howard Johnson Hotel is building 1, and the offices of the Democratic National Committee are indicated by arrows on building 2.

Woodward and Bernstein

When five burglars were first arrested at the Watergate *The Washington Post* assigned two young reporters, twenty-nine-year-old Bob Woodward and twenty-eight-year-old Carl Bernstein, to cover the story. The national staff of the *Post* rarely covered police stories, and that's what Watergate was at first. Woodward and Bernstein were local reporters.

They had never worked together before. In many respects they were very different. Woodward was a graduate of Yale and a veteran of the Navy officer corps. He was well connected in Washington society and with the Washington political establishment. Bernstein was a college dropout who had been a full-time reporter since the age of nineteen. He liked to write long pieces about the capital's neighborhoods and people, and he occasionally reviewed rock music for the *Post*. He was also the better writer.

In other ways they were very much alike. Neither was married, both were ambitious and tenacious. They were willing and able to put in endless hours calling, interviewing, and checking and rechecking the complex story of Watergate. They did so many articles together that people began calling them "Woodstein."

Woodward had a confidential source he called "Deep Throat," who knew a great deal about inside operations at the White House and was able to point the reporters in productive directions. The identity of "Deep Throat" has never been revealed and has been the subject of much speculation.

Reporters for many different papers did excellent investigative reporting on Watergate, but Woodward and Bernstein did the most. And *The Washington Post* became the chief target of the Nixon administration.

The *Post* won a Pulitzer Prize for Woodward and Bernstein's reporting. The pair also wrote two extremely popular and influential books on Watergate, *All the President's Men* and *The Final Days*. In 1976 *All the President's Men* was made into a popular film.

the serial numbers in intriguingly close sequence. A bag of electronic equipment was found in their possession. One of the pieces of equipment was quickly identified as a device used for tapping telephones. They also had a walkie-talkie, pen-sized tear-gas guns, lock picks, forty rolls of unexposed film, and two 35-millimeter cameras.

In the men's pockets were found the keys to a couple of rooms in the Watergate Hotel, which adjoined the office building, a key to a room in the Howard Johnson Motor Inn, directly across from the Watergate, and a bill from the restaurant in the Watergate indicating that before they broke in to the DNC headquarters, they had eaten a very expensive meal in the hotel restaurant. The Washington police sensed that there was something important happening and called in an assistant U.S. attorney and the FBI.

The five arrested men didn't exercise their right to call a lawyer. In the afternoon a couple of prominent Washington attorneys showed up anyway. The press showed up, too, when the five "Watergate burglars," as they came to be called, were brought before a judge for a preliminary hearing.

The judge asked the men their profession. "Anticommunists," one of them replied. The others nodded in agreement. The judge seemed surprised. The judge then asked the tallest of the men to step forward and give his name and profession. To the first question he now truthfully replied, "James McCord." He gave his profession as security consultant, now retired from government service.

The judge asked him what government service.

GOP Security Aide Among 5 Arrested In Bugging Affair

By Bob Woodward and Carl Bernstein

Washington Post Staff Writers

One of the five men arrested early Saturday in the attempt to bug the Democratic National Committee headquarters here is the salaried security coordinator for President Nixon's re-election committee.

The suspect, former CIA employee James W. McCord Jr., 53, also holds a separate contract to provide security services to the Republican National Committee, GOP national chairman Bob Dole said yesterday.

Former Attorney General John N. Mitchell, head of the Committee for the Re-Election of the President, said yesterday McCord was employed to help install that committee's own security system.

In a statement issued in Los Angeles, Mitchell said McCord and the other four men arrested at Democratic headquarters Saturday "were not operating either in our behalf or with our consent" in the alleged bugging attempt.

Dole issued a similar statement, adding that "we deplore action of this kind in or out of politics." An aide to Dole said he was unsure at this time exactly what security services McCord was hired to perform by the National Committee.

Police sources said last night that they were seeking a sixth man in connection with the attempted bugging. The sources would give no other details.

Other sources close to the investigation said yesterday that there still was no explanation as to why the five suspects might have attempted to bug Democratic headquarters in the Watergate at 2600 Virginia Ave. NW, or if they were working for other individuals or organizations.

"We're baffled at this point . . . the mystery deepens," a high Democratic party source said.

Democratic National Committee Chairman Lawrence F. O'Brien said the "bugging incident . . . raised the

JAMES W. McCORD
. . . retired CIA employee

ugliest questions about the integrity of the political process that I have encountered in a quarter century

"No mere statement of innocence by Mr. Nixon's campaign manager will dispel these questions."

The Democratic presidential candidates were not available for comment yesterday.

O'Brien, in his statement, called on Attorney General Richard G. Kleindienst to order an immediate, "search

See ARREST, A6, Col. 1

Bernard Barker, Eugenio R. Martinez, Frank Sturgis and Virgilio R. Gonzales, from left, held in connection with attempt to bug Democratic Committee offices.

The first of many articles by Woodward and Bernstein about the Watergate break-in. They could not have realized at this point that this story would lead them to the offices of the president of the United States.

"CIA," McCord whispered. The mention of the CIA, the Central Intelligence Agency, certainly caught the attention of reporters who were close enough to overhear it.

McCord was also soon recognized as the security chief of the Committee to Reelect the President (CRP, or CREEP, as it came to be called). This was a committee set up to promote the reelection of President Richard M. Nixon. CRP headquarters was just across the street from the White House.

There was more. Among the effects found on the men were two address books with the name and phone number of E. Howard Hunt, with the small notation "W. House" or "W.H." It was quickly discovered that Howard Hunt was another former CIA man who had some sort of job at the White House.

Investigators began to uncover more and more links between the Watergate burglars and the Nixon administration. Over the next four months, stories about these links began to appear regularly in the press, particularly in *The Washington Post*. Lawrence O'Brien, chairman of the Democratic National Committee, in whose offices the burglars had been found, said that the break-in "raised the ugliest question about the integrity of the political process that I have encountered in a quarter of a century of political activity."

President Nixon, on the other hand, dismissed the break-in as "a bizarre incident," of no political significance. The public at large didn't seem to care very much.

The year 1972 was a presidential election year. A badly split Democratic party nominated Senator George McGovern, a staunch opponent of the war in Vietnam, as their candidate. The Republicans nominated Richard Nixon for a second term. His slogan was "Four More Years!"

The Democratic campaign got off to a horrible start, as McGovern was forced to drop one vice-presidential nominee and pick another. After that the campaign never got off the ground, and as the election neared it was clear that Nixon was headed for an election victory of historic proportions.

Watergate never became an issue. It was barely even mentioned during the campaign.

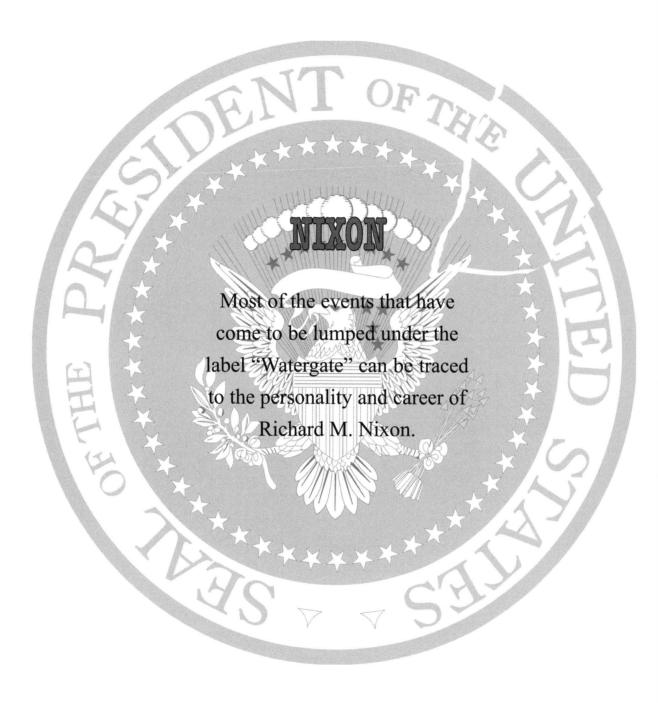

Most of the events that have
come to be lumped under the
label "Watergate" can be traced
to the personality and career of
Richard M. Nixon.

By 1972 Nixon had been part of the American political scene for a long time. He first ran for Congress in 1946 as a Republican from his home district in California. His opponent was Democratic congressman Jerry Voorhis. Nixon based his campaign on the charge that the liberal Voorhis was "soft on communism." Nixon was swept into office in a Republican tide.

In the House of Representatives, Nixon quickly established himself as one of the most vigorous anticommunists. By 1950 he was ready to run for the U.S. Senate. This time his opponent was the popular California congresswoman Helen Gahagan Douglas, a liberal Democrat and former actress. Nixon dubbed her "the pink lady," thus labeling her as a Communist or red sympathizer. Nixon won a landslide victory and became, at age thirty-six, the youngest member of the Senate.

In 1952 the Republicans nominated General Dwight D. Eisenhower as their presidential candidate. "Ike," as he was called, was from the moderate wing of the party, and lived on the East Coast. To balance the ticket the Republicans nominated Nixon, a Californian, and a rising young star with impeccable right-wing credentials, for vice president.

The Eisenhower/Nixon ticket was headed for certain victory when, in September 1952 the press revealed that several wealthy Californians had secretly contributed more than $18,000 for Nixon while he was in the Senate. This wasn't strictly illegal. But it looked very bad, particularly for a candidate who had been campaigning hard against Democratic corruption.

There were calls for Nixon to resign as vice-presidential candidate. Nixon fought back. He went on national television and

DOUGLAS-MARCANTONIO VOTING RECORD

Many persons have requested a comparison of the voting records of Congresswoman Helen Douglas and the notorious Communist party-liner, Congressman Vito Marcantonio of New York.

Mrs. Douglas and Marcantonio have been members of Congress together since January 1, 1945. During that period, Mrs. Douglas voted the same as Marcantonio **354** times. While it should not be expected that a member of the House of Representatives should always vote in opposition to Marcantonio, it is significant to note, not only the great number of times which Mrs. Douglas voted in agreement with him, but also the issues on which almost without exception they always saw eye to eye, to-wit: Un-American Activities and Internal Security.

Here is the Record!

VOTES AGAINST COMMITTEE ON UN-AMERICAN ACTIVITIES

Both Douglas and Marcantonio voted **against** establishing the Committee on Un-American Activities. 1/3/45. Bill passed.

Both voted on three separate occasions **against** contempt proceedings against persons and organizations which refused to reveal records or answer whether they were Communists. 4/16/46, 6/26/46, 11/24/47. Bills passed.

Both voted on four separate occasions **against** allowing funds for investigation by the Un-American Activities Committee. 5/17/46, 5/9/48, 2/9/49, 3/23/50. (The last vote was 348 to 12.) All bills passed.

COMMUNIST-LINE FOREIGN POLICY VOTES

Both voted **against** Greek-Turkish Aid Bill. 5/9/47. (It has been established that without this aid Greece and Turkey would long since have gone behind the Iron Curtain.) Bill passed.

Both voted on two occasions **against** free press amendment to UNRRA appropriation bill, providing that no funds should be furnished any country which refused to allow free access to the news of activities of the United States. 11/1/45, 6/28/46. Bills passed. (This would in effect have denied American relief funds to Communist dominated countries.)

Both voted **against** refusing Foreign Relief to Soviet-dominated countries UNLESS supervised by Americans. 4/30/47. Bill passed 324 to 75.

VOTE AGAINST NATIONAL DEFENSE

Both voted **against** the Selective Service Act of 1948. 6/18/48. Bill passed.

VOTES AGAINST LOYALTY AND SECURITY LEGISLATION

Both voted on two separate occasions **against** bills requiring loyalty checks for Federal employees. 7/15/47, 6/29/49. Bills passed.

Both voted **against** the Subversive Activities Control Act of 1948, requiring registration with the Attorney General of Communist party members and communist controlled organizations. Bill passed, 319 to 58. 5/19/48. **AND AFTER KOREA** both again voted against it. Bill passed 8/29/50, 354 to 20.

AFTER KOREA, on July 12, 1950, Marcantonio and Douglas and 12 others voted **against** the Security Bill, to permit the heads of key National Defense departments, such as the Atomic Energy Commission, to discharge government workers found to be poor security risks! Bill passed, 327 to 14.

VOTE AGAINST CALIFORNIA

Both recorded **against** confirming title to Tidelands in California and the other states affected. 4/30/48. Bill passed 257-29.

VOTES AGAINST CONGRESSIONAL INVESTIGATION OF COMMUNIST AND OTHER ILLEGAL ACTIVITIES

Both voted **against** investigating the "whitewash" of the AMERASIA case. 4/18/46. Bill passed.

Both voted **against** investigating why the Soviet Union was buying as many as 60,000 United States patents at one time. 3/4/47. Bill passed.

Both voted **against** continuing investigation of numerous instances of illegal actions by OPA and the War Labor Board. 1/18/45. Bill passed.

Both voted on two occasions **against** allowing Congress to have access to government records necessary to the conduct of investigations by Senate and House Committees. 4/22/48, 5/13/48. Bills passed.

ON ALL OF THE ABOVE VOTES which have occurred since Congressman Nixon took office on January 1, 1947, HE has voted exactly opposite to the Douglas-Marcantonio Axis!

After studying the voting comparison between Mrs. Douglas and Marcantonio, is it any wonder that the Communist line newspaper, the Daily People's World, in its lead editorial on January 31, 1950, labeled Congressman Nixon as "The Man To Beat" in this Senate race and that the Communist newspaper, the New York Daily Worker, in the issue of July 28, 1947, selected Mrs. Douglas along with Marcantonio as "One of the Heroes of the 80th Congress."

REMEMBER! The United States Senate votes on ratifying international treaties and confirming presidential appointments. Would California send Marcantonio to the United States Senate?

NIXON FOR U. S. SENATOR CAMPAIGN COMMITTEE

NORTHERN CALIFORNIA
John Walton Dinkelspiel, Chairman
1151 Market Street
San Francisco—UNderhill 3-1416

CENTRAL CALIFORNIA
B. M. Hoblick, Chairman
820 Van Ness Avenue
Fresno—Phone 44116

SOUTHERN CALIFORNIA
Bernard Brennan, C
117 W. 9th St., L
TRinity 0061

This is the handbill put together by Nixon and his campaign committee to slander California Congresswoman Helen Douglas. A careful study of her voting record revealed that this so-called "pink" sheet was a complete fraud.

A bumper sticker from the campaign of 1952.

declared he had done nothing wrong. It was an emotional appeal in which he talked about everything from his wife's "cloth coat" to a cocker spaniel named Checkers that had been given to his children. It was dubbed the "Checkers speech" and was a huge success. Letters and telegrams of support poured in. Again, the Republicans won a landslide victory.

For eight years Nixon served loyally and effectively as vice president, though Eisenhower never really liked Nixon and gave him little of importance to do. Still, Nixon expected that his service would be rewarded with the presidency.

While Nixon was politically effective, he was never popular. Unlike Eisenhower, who was liked even by people who disagreed with him, Nixon made a lot of enemies. In public he often appeared stiff and awkward. His hard-driving, anything-to-win political style had earned him the title "Tricky Dick." It was a label he could never shake.

When Nixon first ran for president in 1960 he had the misfortune to run against a charismatic young Democratic congressman from Massachusetts named John F. Kennedy. Nationally, Kennedy was a political unknown and Nixon was favored to win. Then he faced Kennedy in a series of televised debates. Kennedy was articulate, cool, and telegenic. Nixon was well informed and a good debater, but he looked uncomfortable and shifty-eyed. Kennedy won the debates and the election by the narrowest of margins. Republicans claimed that Kennedy had "stolen" the election with voting frauds in Chicago. That often-repeated charge backfired and gave Nixon the reputation of being a sore loser.

Nixon returned to California, his political career apparently over. But in 1962 he tried a comeback by running for governor. He accused incumbent governor Pat Brown of being dangerously left-wing. This tactic that had worked for him so often in the past had no effect. Nixon was badly defeated. When he came to deliver his concession speech, he was not gracious in defeat. He blamed the press in a bitter, rambling diatribe:

"Just think how much you're going to be missing. You won't have Nixon to kick around anymore, because gentlemen, this is my last press conference."

Throughout the speech Nixon, rumpled and unshaven, looked almost out of control. Absolutely everyone agreed that this performance ended any chance he might have had of another political comeback.

And everyone was wrong. After a few years Nixon once again immersed himself in Republican politics. He campaigned for Republican candidates, raised money, and in 1968 he once again got the Republican presidential nomination.

The Democratic nominee was Vice President Hubert Humphrey. The Democratic party was practically at war with itself over the unpopular war in Vietnam. President Lyndon Johnson had escalated the war. As a loyal vice president, Humphrey had supported the policy. This made him a target for the large and vocal antiwar segment of the Democratic Party. There were riots at the 1968 Democratic party convention in Chicago. Richard

Nixon won a narrow victory, but it was a victory capping the most remarkable political comeback in American history.

During his first term Nixon presented himself as "the new Nixon," a mature statesman no longer consumed by the anger and vindictiveness he had shown in the past. There were notable accomplishments, particularly his visit to Communist China, which opened relations with the most populous nation on earth. It was a bold move, and one that Nixon would have denounced as very nearly treasonous, had it been undertaken by a Democratic president.

Within Washington itself, though, information that the Nixon Administration found embarrassing or damaging was constantly being leaked to the press, and there seemed no way of stopping it. As his concession speech of "You won't have Nixon to kick around" indicated, Richard Nixon had always distrusted the press.

There were other problems as well, particularly the war in Vietnam. During the 1968 election campaign, Nixon had promised to bring that disastrous and unpopular conflict to an end. But it dragged on. Protests and student demonstrations against the war were increasing. Nixon and his inner circle felt that much of this protest was being organized by the Communists—but the regular investigative bodies like the FBI couldn't come up with the sort of information he wanted.

Many Republicans were defeated in the 1970 mid-term elections, and the president faced not only a Democratic but an increasingly hostile Congress.

Finally, Nixon began to believe that all of this would play into the hands of the Democrats and hurt his reelection chances.

Something had to be done.

THE PLUMBERS

When Richard Nixon was elected president in 1968 he carried all his old resentments and fears with him. The president, and many of those around him, had difficulty in seeing the difference between legitimate political opposition and threats, communist or otherwise, to the nation. Sometimes they could see no difference at all.

Kent State University, May 4, 1970. During an antiwar protest, National Guard troops shot and killed four students. These deaths stirred the antiwar movement to even greater heights.

Nixon and many of his associates always believed that the anti-Vietnam war movement in the United States was being orchestrated by the Communists, although there was no evidence to support this.

On May 4, 1970, four students at Kent State University in Ohio were shot to death by Ohio National Guardsmen during an antiwar demonstration. Two more students were killed by the police at Jackson State University, Mississippi, during a similar demonstration.

A few days after the Kent State shootings a massive student demonstration was planned for Washington, D.C. As the students began to arrive the night before the demonstration, the usually reserved Nixon did something completely uncharacteristic. In the middle of the night, with only a small Secret Service detail, he went out to where some of the students had gathered to talk to them. The president was emotional but he did not address the main points of the student protest. No minds were changed. Nixon was upset because the press treated this episode as an oddity, rather than an expression of his feelings of concern for the students.

On Sunday, June 13, 1971, *The New York Times* began publishing a massive military study of U.S. involvement in the war in Vietnam. The study documented in great detail the mistakes that the U.S. government had made, and the lies the government had told. The study, which came to be known as the Pentagon Papers, was supposed to have been secret. It had been leaked to the press by Daniel Ellsberg, a former government official and one-time supporter of the war who had become thoroughly disillusioned.

The Pentagon Papers covered events that occurred during previous, mostly Democratic, administrations. They contained no information about what the Nixon administration was doing. But they clearly provided ammunition for the antiwar movement. To the Nixon administration, they came to represent the ultimate antiwar propaganda. Leaking the Pentagon Papers was viewed by the White House as being tantamount to treason.

The Nixon administration had already been pressing investigative agencies, the FBI and CIA, to supply more intelligence about antiwar groups, and about opponents of the administration in general. Some of the methods proposed for gathering information, such as breaking in to the homes and offices of those being investigated, were clearly illegal. Opposition came from a most surprising source, FBI Director J. Edgar Hoover.

Hoover had been head of the FBI since 1924. He had accumulated enormous power and prestige and was virtually untouchable. He was also one of Richard Nixon's great heroes. Hoover was a rabid anticommunist. In the past he had not hesitated to use illegal means in an attempt to trap those he thought were inspired by communism, or otherwise threatened his view of the American way of life.

No one is quite sure why Hoover opposed the administration's plans. He seemed to think that some of the suggestions were reckless. If the activities were exposed they could damage the reputation of the FBI. Hoover also feared that cooperation with the CIA would undermine the independence of the Bureau. And he didn't like being ordered around by members of the White House staff. Some in the Nixon administration thought Hoover had become "senile." Whatever his reasons, Hoover's opposition doomed any administration plans.

President Nixon with FBI Director J. Edgar Hoover in 1971.

Since the regular agencies couldn't be used, the Nixon administration decided to set up its own secret investigative agency, run from the White House. The agency was given the name "the Plumbers," because one of its main tasks was to stop "leaks" to the news media.

Planning for a vast array of illegal activities went on at the very highest level of the Nixon administration. Those involved included John Mitchell, attorney general of the United States, and later director of Nixon's 1972 reelection campaign; Charles Colson, special White House counsel, and generally regarded as Nixon's "hatchet man"; John Ehrlichman, chief domestic policy

E. Howard Hunt, Jr.

G. Gordon Liddy

adviser to the president; and H. R. "Bob" Haldeman, White House chief of staff and, next to the president, the most powerful man in the administration. Finally, there was President Richard Nixon himself. He not only set the "I don't care how it's done" attitude for his staff, he directly participated in discussions and decisions that led to illegal activities by his subordinates.

Among those employed by the Plumbers was E. Howard Hunt, a semi-retired CIA agent and prolific writer of spy thrillers. Another was G. Gordon Liddy, an eccentric former assistant district attorney who regarded himself as a soldier in the war against communism, and who said he was willing to do anything, no matter how illegal, that his commander-in-chief ordered him to do.

One of the Plumbers' goals was to try and discredit Senator Edward (Ted) Kennedy, a possible presidential rival for 1972. Ever since his defeat by John Kennedy, Nixon had hated and feared the Kennedy clan. Hunt produced fake State Department cables indicating that President John Kennedy and other members of his administration had been involved in the assassination of a president of South Vietnam. Nixon associate Charles Colson then tried to have the news media publish a damaging exposé of the Kennedy administration based on the fake cables. The story was never published and the forgeries were put back in Howard Hunt's safe in the White House.

After the Pentagon Papers began appearing in the press, a chief aim of the Nixon administration was to discredit the man who had leaked the papers, Daniel Ellsberg. Ellsberg had been treated by a California psychiatrist, Dr. Lewis Fielding. Hunt and Liddy were directed to break into Dr. Fielding's office to see if they could find any damaging information on Ellsberg in the doctor's files. To help with the break-in Hunt recruited several anti-Castro Cuban Americans whom he had known from his CIA days.

The break-in took place on September 3, 1971, but no Ellsberg files could be found. Hunt and Liddy thought that the psychiatrist might have taken the files home, and suggested a break-in there. This plan was never carried out.

Liddy had proposed a number of actions to disrupt opponents of the Nixon administration. These included everything from bugging the offices and phones of Democratic candidates and officials to the assassination of Washington columnist Jack Anderson, who had been publishing a lot of damaging information about administration activities. Later Liddy was to claim that he was just kidding when he made the assassination suggestion. But some of those who heard him thought he was serious. He was never reprimanded and he was never fired.

On the contrary, Liddy and Hunt were given new powers and a new assignment. They were to burglarize the office of the Democratic National Committee in the Watergate, and place a listening device in the phone of DNC chairman Lawrence O'Brien. O'Brien, an old friend of the Kennedy's, had always been considered a particularly dangerous political opponent by Richard Nixon.

To do the job Hunt again called on the services of the Cubans who had helped in the break-in at Dr. Fielding's office. They recruited electronics specialist James McCord, a former CIA agent currently employed as security chief by the Republican National Committee and the Committee to Reelect the President. Also in on the operation was Alfred Baldwin, a former FBI agent working for CRP.

For all their experience, the men of the Hunt-Liddy team were incompetent burglars. In June they made several unsuccessful attempts to get into Democratic headquarters. They actually did get in once and installed bugging equipment, but it didn't work. So on the night of June 16 they tried again.

This time they got caught.

THE COVER-UP

On the surface everything looked secure for Richard Nixon. In November 1972, he and his vice presidential running mate, Spiro Agnew, cruised to a landslide victory. The Republican slate took 60.7 percent of the popular vote. The electoral college vote was even more lopsided, 520 for Nixon and a mere 17 for Democrat George McGovern.

Watergate had never figured as a campaign issue. Even the Democrats had failed to exploit it. Inside the White House, however, the president and his top advisers were very worried. Only they knew the full story of Watergate, and only they knew how much damage could be done if it was revealed.

Later Jeb Magruder, deputy director of the President's reelection campaign recalled: "At some point that Saturday morning [after the break-in] I realized that this was not just hard-nosed politics, this was a crime that could destroy us all. The cover-up, thus, was immediate and automatic; no one ever considered that there would *not* be a cover-up. It seemed inconceivable that with our political power we could not erase this mistake we had made." The shredding and burning of potentially incriminating documents at the White House and the Committee to Reelect the President began at once.

Howard Hunt had a safe at the White House. The day after the arrests the contents of the safe were delivered to John Dean, a young lawyer who was counsel to the president. Dean quickly assumed a central role in the cover-up. Dean and his assistant, wearing surgical gloves to avoid leaving fingerprints, went through the contents. Among other things they found a loaded revolver, McCord's leftover bugging equipment, material on Daniel Ellsberg, and copies of the State Department cables that Hunt had fabricated. This was potential political dynamite, and Dean knew it.

Five men had been arrested inside the DNC. Two more, Hunt and Liddy, had been identified as directing the break-in from the Howard Johnson's across the street, and also were arrested later.

They were all facing the possibility of long jail sentences. The first priority was to make sure that none of them began talking. The four Cubans knew relatively little. McCord knew more and Hunt and Liddy knew enough to unravel the entire plot.

Next, investigations by the Washington police, the FBI, federal prosecutors, and—increasingly—the press had to be deflected or derailed somehow. And down the road there was Congress. Despite the Nixon landslide, both houses of Congress remained firmly in the hands of the Democrats. Congress had broad powers to investigate suspected wrongdoing in government.

While the Nixon administration did not have absolute power over the investigation, it did have considerable influence. The attorney general, the nation's chief law enforcement officer was Richard Kleindienst, a Nixon loyalist. Immediately after the first arrests, Liddy contacted Kleindienst. He explained the situation and wanted to get his men out of jail. Kleindienst said that was impossible because it would raise too many questions. But he was the nation's chief law enforcement officer. He had been given the details of illegal activities, and he did nothing but shake hands with the man who had planned the burglary. Kleindienst was later to participate in meetings where the cover-up was discussed.

The troublesome J. Edgar Hoover had died in May 1972. He was replaced by another Nixon loyalist, L. Patrick Gray, who was appointed acting FBI director. Still another Nixon man, General Vernon Walters, was made deputy director of the CIA. These men had great power to limit and deflect any investigation. And they used it.

Spiro Agnew

Spiro Agnew had been the Republican governor of Maryland before Richard Nixon chose him as his vice-presidential running mate. Agnew didn't have a particularly distinguished political career, but he was a good speaker with a sharp tongue. During the 1968 campaign he got the reputation of being "Nixon's Nixon." He made the slashing attacks, while Nixon himself tried to look presidential.

Nixon and Agnew were never close. As his Watergate troubles mounted, Nixon began to regard Agnew as his "impeachment insurance." He reasoned that the Democrats wouldn't want to get rid of him because then they would have Agnew, whom they disliked even more.

Agnew was untainted by Watergate, but he had his own scandals to contend with. Prosecutors in Baltimore had uncovered evidence that while governor, he had accepted bribes from contractors and others who did business with the state. He continued to take cash bribes in plain envelopes in his White House office in the Executive Office Building after he became vice president.

Facing prosecution as a common criminal, and a long prison sentence, Agnew made a bargain with prosecutors. He would resign as vice president in exchange for a recommendation of leniency from the attorney general.

On October 10, 1973, Agnew pleaded no contest to the charge of income tax evasion and was given a suspended sentence and a ten-thousand dollar fine. Earlier in the day he sent a one sentence letter of resignation to the Secretary of State.

Two days later Nixon appointed Republican House Minority Leader Gerald Ford as his choice for vice president. Ford was an amiable man, well liked by his colleagues in both parties. He was quickly and easily confirmed by the Senate.

The most immediate problem was the situation of those already arrested for the burglary. They faced U.S. District Court Chief Judge John J. Sirica. Sirica had been nicknamed "Maximum John" for his habit of handing out the toughest possible sentences. He would often use the threat of long sentences to get defendants who he thought were lying to start telling the truth. It was obvious that Judge Sirica thought the Watergate defendants were telling a lot less than the full truth. He wanted to know why these men had gone into Democratic headquarters. Were they paid? Who hired them? Who had started all of this?

The first White House reaction was to publicly try to downplay the whole affair. As soon as the Watergate arrests were announced, presidential spokesman Ron Ziegler characterized the incident as "a third-rate burglary attempt," not worth dignifying with further comment.

The next line of defense was that it was a "caper" that had been dreamed up entirely by the Cuban Americans. When that crumbled there was an attempt to keep the investigations from going any further by claiming that Liddy had organized the whole thing on his own. Liddy was willing, even eager, to take all the blame. Federal prosecutors, who reported to the attorney general, seemed willing to accept that explanation. But Sirica wouldn't buy it. He kept on pressing.

A more promising approach was to try and limit the investigation by saying that pushing too far would expose secret CIA activities and thus endanger "national security." Gray and Walters met several times to discuss this approach. "Protecting national security" became one of the main themes during the early months of the cover-up.

The press, particularly *The Washington Post*, pursued the intriguing Watergate story aggressively. At first they had no idea how big it would be. The most productive line of inquiry was "the money trail." Reporters were able to discover that the money used to pay for the Watergate break-in, and for a host of other nasty political dirty tricks, came directly from the Committee to Reelect the President. More than two million dollars in cash from unreported campaign contributions was stored in safes and safety deposit boxes in CRP headquarters and elsewhere.

After the election the tempo of the Watergate investigation began to pick up. On March 19, 1973, came the first major break. McCord, facing a long jail sentence, sent a letter to Judge Sirica admitting that he and other defendants had committed perjury—they had lied—and that high officials at the White House not only knew about the Watergate break-in—they had ordered it.

UNRAVELING

The seven men charged with
the Watergate burglary went
on trial January 8, 1973.
After a sixteen-day trial all
the defendants were found
guilty of burglary, conspiracy,
and illegal wiretapping.

John J. Sirica, then the chief district court judge in Washington. He is shown here in his office after signing a show cause order. The Nixon administration had two weeks to tell why it shouldn't have to supply special prosecutor Archibald Cox with the tapes Nixon had made of his conversations in the Oval Office.

Judge Sirica wasn't satisfied. He felt that the prosecutors had not pressed hard enough. Too many fundamental and obvious questions remained unanswered. He delayed sentencing until March 23. On March 20, McCord walked into the judge's chambers and handed his clerk a letter. When Sirica read the letter he told his clerk, "This is going to break the case wide open."

On March 23, Sirica read the letter in open court. Among the points McCord made in his letter were:

- Political pressure had been applied to the defendants to plead guilty and remain silent.

- Perjury had occurred frequently during the trial.

- Others involved in Watergate were not identified during the trial, though they could have been.

- The Watergate operation had nothing to do with the CIA.

McCord also stated that members of his family had expressed fear for his life if he told what he knew, and that he did not feel confident talking to the FBI, to a grand jury controlled by U.S. attorneys working for the Department of Justice, or to any other government representative. He did, however, make it clear he would be willing to talk to a congressional committee.

That option was now available. On February 7, 1973, the Senate voted to create a select committee to investigate Watergate. Chosen as committee chairman was Senator Sam Ervin of North Carolina, a moderately conservative southern Democrat. Public hearings were to begin in May.

True to his reputation, Judge Sirica imposed heavy sentences on the other Watergate defendants, but indicated that he would shorten their sentences if they cooperated fully with the Ervin Committee.

Howard Hunt was close to the breaking point. In December his wife, Dorothy, had been killed in a plane crash. She had been carrying $10,000 in cash, part of the money Hunt had been paid to keep quiet. Her death shattered him. He also began to feel as if the White House was going back on its commitments for more money and a promise of clemency after serving only a small part of his sentence. He hinted to John Ehrlichman that he had done "seamy" things for the White House that he could talk about if his demands were not met.

There was, however, an even more important—and for the Nixon administration, more dangerous—potential witness. John

John W. Dean III on his second day of testimony. Dean told the Watergate Committee that he believed President Nixon probably knew about the planning of the Watergate break-in and definitely participated in the cover-up.

Dean, Nixon's young personal counsel, had been intimately involved in the cover-up from the time it began. While others might have heard about the involvement of higher-ups, that was only hearsay. Dean had first-hand knowledge of practically everything, including the actions of the president.

Nixon had publicly announced that Dean had conducted a thorough investigation and found that no one in the White House was involved in Watergate, and that Dean was writing a full report on his investigation. Dean knew this wasn't true. He saw the defenses crumbling all around him and was afraid that he was being set up as the scapegoat to protect the president and his top aides. They could say that Dean had engineered the entire cover-up, and had kept vital information from them. By the end of March, Dean had secretly hired his own lawyer and began negotiating with prosecutors and the staff of the Ervin Committee.

Nixon had his own strategy for handling the committee. He told John Mitchell, "I want you all to stonewall it, let them plead the

Fifth Amendment, cover-up or anything else, if it'll save it—save the plan. . . Up to this point, the whole theory has been containment, as you know, John."

On April 30, Nixon went on national television to announce that his two top aides, Bob Haldeman and John Ehrlichman, were resigning. He called them "two of the finest public servants it has been my privilege to know." Attorney General Kleindienst, he said, was resigning because he did not want to be placed in the position of possibly prosecuting people who had been his friends. And finally, he said that John Dean had been fired.

The New York Times, Tuesday, May 1, 1973. Nixon is fifteen months away from resigning the presidency, and trying hard to contain the damage.

The Ervin Committee began the public phase of its hearings on May 16. They were fully televised and riveted the nation. Chairman Sam Ervin was a heavy-set, baggy-faced man with a deceptively folksy manner. He immediately became a popular favorite. Haldeman, Ehrlichman, and Mitchell came across as arrogant and deceitful. There were too many things they conveniently couldn't recall.

John Dean finally testified on June 25. For two days he read his carefully prepared statement, laying out in great detail what led up to Watergate and the cover-up that followed. He was questioned for four more days—but his testimony remained unshaken.

One of Dean's more startling revelations was that he had given some of the more damaging materials found in Howard Hunt's safe to acting FBI Director L. Patrick Gray with the instruction that the material should never see the light of day. Ehrlichman said that if ever asked they could say the material had been "given to the FBI." Gray had kept the material at his Connecticut home for several months, then burned it with the Christmas trash. The head of the FBI had personally destroyed evidence.

Dean may not have been likable—he was testifying to save his own skin—but he was believable. Senator Howard Baker, senior Republican on the committee, asked Dean what became the central question of the Watergate hearings, "What did the president know, and when did he know it?" According to Dean, the president knew everything, and he knew it from the start.

As damning as Dean's testimony was, at this point it was really his word against Nixon's. All that was to change on July 14.

TAPES

Bob Woodward of *The Washington Post*
got the dramatic news this way. On Saturday,
July 14, he received a call at home from a
member of the Ervin Committee staff.
"Congratulations," he said. "We interviewed
Butterfield. He told the whole story."

"What whole story?"

"Nixon bugged himself."

Alexander Butterfield was a minor White House functionary. He took care of the president's schedule. On July 13, he was being given a routine interview by the committee staff in a closed session when he revealed that the Nixon White House had an extensive taping system. Virtually all of the conversations that Nixon had were taped. Very few had known of the existence of the taping system, and before Butterfield, no one had mentioned it.

This was sensational news. Now John Dean's version of events could be tested against Richard Nixon's.

On Monday, Butterfield appeared at the public hearing as a surprise witness. He testified for only half an hour. But what he said about the taping system completely changed the focus of Watergate. From that moment on it became primarily a fight over the tapes.

After Kleindienst resigned as attorney general, Nixon appointed Elliot Richardson to fill the post. Richardson was a Republican, but not a hard-core Nixon loyalist. Congress had given the attorney general the power to appoint a special prosecutor, who would work independently of the Justice Department, to investigate Watergate. Richardson appointed Archibald Cox, a Harvard law professor, who had served in the Kennedy administration.

When the news that tapes of the president's conversations existed was revealed, Cox immediately tried to obtain those tapes that might be relevant to his investigation. Nixon flatly refused, citing the doctrine of "executive privilege"—the president had the right to protect the content of his private conversations.

Nixon offered a variety of compromises short of turning over the recordings themselves, but Cox was adamant. Finally, on Saturday, October 20, Nixon decided to end the controversy. He ordered Richardson to fire Cox. Richardson had promised Cox complete independence. He refused the president's order and resigned. Deputy Attorney General William Ruckelshaus was then ordered to fire the special prosecutor. He, too, refused and resigned. The third highest official at the Justice Department, Robert Bork, did agree to fire Cox. The incident became known as the Saturday Night Massacre.

Nixon may have believed that with Cox gone his troubles would be over. He wanted the powers of the special prosecutor returned to the Justice Department. But it didn't turn out that way. The president's new chief of staff, General Alexander Haig, ordered the FBI to seal the offices of the special prosecutor and those of Richardson and Ruckelshaus. Henry Ruth, Cox's chief deputy, was not allowed to enter his own office. He told the assembled reporters, "One thinks in a democracy maybe this would not happen. . ." Haig's move was a public-relations disaster.

The Saturday Night Massacre provoked a firestorm of protest. Millions of messages poured into the White House and Congress. Telephone and telegraph lines couldn't handle the volume. Most of the messages opposed the president's action. The Nixon administration couldn't stand up to that kind of pressure. Within a few days they were forced to appoint a new special prosecutor. He was Leon Jaworski, a Texas lawyer. Jaworski was a Democrat who had supported Nixon in the last election. He was given even more independence than Cox had, and he kept Cox's staff of aggressive young prosecutors. The

"There you have it—the unbelievable Rose Mary Woods with a record 18 minutes in the tape erasure medleys—now to Jim with the demolition derby in Bayonne...."

This cartoon by Doug Marlette of *The Charlotte Observer* reflected the humor many people found in Rose Mary Woods explanations of how she erased eighteen critical minutes from a tape recording.

Watergate investigation continued with hardly a pause. Not only had the move to get rid of the special prosecutor failed, it made things worse for Richard Nixon. That, combined with Nixon's refusal to hand over the tapes, and the press's continued attention to that point, led to serious discussions for the first time that the president might be impeached.

In response to pressure from Judge Sirica, Nixon slowly and grudgingly began to turn over some of the tapes demanded by Jaworski. But some of the tapes were missing. Nixon claimed that for one reason or another these conversations had not been recorded. Most damaging of all was the revelation that the tape of an important conversation between Nixon and Haldeman contained a highly suspicious eighteen-minute gap. Rose Mary Woods, the president's fiercely loyal long-time secretary, said that she might have accidentally erased part of the tape when she was transcribing it. That explanation was widely ridiculed.

On November 17, Richard Nixon went on live television to defend himself from the snowballing charges. He made what would become the most widely quoted statement of his long political career: "People have to know whether or not their president is a crook. Well, I am not a crook."

ENDGAME

On February 25, 1974, the grand jury that had been
considering Watergate voted to indict seven former
Nixon aides, some of whom had been among the most
powerful men in government, for conspiracy to obstruct
justice and a host of other crimes.

There was also a secret section to the indictment. In
this the grand jury determined that there was "probable
cause" to believe that Richard M. Nixon was a
member of the conspiracy. He was named as an
"unindicted co-conspirator."

Congress had already announced that for only the second time in American history, "formal preparations for impeachment proceedings" against a president had begun. The matter was in the hands of the House Judiciary Committee and its chairman, Peter Rodino of New Jersey. The tone of the debate in Congress indicated that if the president did not turn over all the tapes that were requested, then Republican congressmen "would not go to the wall" for him over impeachment.

Nixon and his staff tried a variety of strategies to keep the damaging information the tapes contained from becoming public. The boldest move was the release of edited transcripts. On April 29, Nixon went on television to announce that he was making public transcripts of forty-six taped conversations. The transcripts had been edited to remove what he said was material unrelated to Watergate, and any profanity. Objectionable words were replaced with the words "expletive deleted." There were loads of expletives deleted in the transcripts, and the phrase became a popular joke.

The move backfired disastrously. Even though the edited transcripts contained no "smoking gun" revelations, the tone of the conversations was petty and sordid. Instead of the dignity that is supposed to be associated with the presidency, here was a group of men sounding like small-time crooks trying to weasel their way out of a mess. And people tended to believe that what had been left out was even worse than what had been left in.

Jaworski wasn't going to be satisfied with edited transcripts, either. He demanded the original tapes. So did the House Judiciary Committee. The president's lawyers argued that neither the

Impeachment

The Constitution provides that a president can be removed from office for "Treason, Bribery or other high Crimes and Misdemeanors." The framers of the Constitution left the phrase deliberately vague. The process is quite clear. The House begins the proceedings by passing resolutions of impeachment, listing the charges. But impeachment does not remove a president. The impeached president then goes on trial before the Senate. The Chief Justice of the Supreme Court presides over the trial. "Managers" appointed by the House act as prosecutors. The president does not appear at the trial. He is represented by counsel. Conviction requires a two-thirds vote by the Senate, and the punishment is removal from office.

President Andrew Johnson was impeached and tried by the Senate in 1868. But by a single vote the Senate failed to find him guilty.

Richard Nixon was never tried. He wasn't even formally impeached. A House committee recommended impeachment, but Nixon resigned before there was a vote in the full House. So no U.S. president has ever actually been removed from office.

courts nor Congress had any constitutional right to the private conversations of the nation's chief executive. On May 31, the U.S. Supreme Court agreed to hear the case of *United States of America* v. *Richard M. Nixon, President.* Hearings were set for July 8.

In June, Richard Nixon departed on an extended foreign trip. Foreign affairs had always been the area of his greatest achievements, and he hoped to refocus public attention on his accomplishments. Nixon received a tumultuous reception in Egypt. But back home the trip had no effect on his popularity. The House Judiciary Committee went ahead preparing for hearings and a vote on impeachment.

On July 24, the very day that the televised debates of the Rodino Committee were to begin, the Supreme Court handed down its decision—the President had to turn over the tapes. The vote was 8–0. Associate Justice William Rehnquist disqualified himself because he had worked for John Mitchell in the Justice Department. Nixon had hoped that if there had been a split ruling he could claim it was not definitive, and not have to comply. The unanimous ruling gave him no room to maneuver. Some of his advisers suggested he destroy the tapes and then resign. Nixon hesitated for eight hours before he announced he would abide by the ruling.

The televised hearings of the Judiciary Committee lasted six days. They did not provide the high drama of the Ervin Committee. They were mostly a sober discussion of legal points. The conclusion was never in doubt. Democrats dominated the committee and would vote to recommend impeachment to the full House. The only questions were exactly what charges would be made and how large the vote margin would be. Some moderate Republicans announced they were going to vote for impeachment. So did the few conservative southern Democrats whom Nixon had counted on. The final vote was 27 to 11.

And there was more bad news for Nixon. After a delay, the tapes were finally turned over on August 5. Among them was the

JUNE 23, 1972 FROM 10:04 TO 11:39 AM

PRESIDENT: When you get in these people . . .
              when you get these people in, say:
              "Look, the problem is that this
              will open the whole, the whole Bay
              of Pigs thing, and the President
              just feels that" ah, without going
              into the details . . . don't, don't
              lie to them to the extent to say
              there is no involvement, but just
              say this is sort of a comedy of
              errors, bizarre, without getting
              into it, "the President believes
              that it is going to open the whole
              Bay of Pigs thing up again. And, ah
              because these people are plugging
              for, for keeps and that they should
              call the FBI in and say that we
              wish for the country, don't go any
              further into this case", period!
HALDEMAN: OK
PRESIDENT: That's the way to put it, do it
              straight. (Unintelligible)
HALDEMAN: Get more done for our cause by the
              opposition than by us at this
              point.
PRESIDENT: You think so?
HALDEMAN: I think so, yeah.

This passage from the original transcripts proved that Nixon knew about the break-in from the very beginning. The transcripts were also shocking to the American public because of the language and the tawdry tone of the Oval Office discussions. An enduring legacy of Watergate is that never again have Americans viewed their leaders with the same degree of respect that they once did.

recording of a June 23, 1972, conversation between Nixon and Haldeman. Just six days after the Watergate break-in, the president and his top aide were discussing ways they could cover up their involvement in it. This was the "smoking gun." It answered the question about what the president knew and when he knew it—and showed even to his most devoted followers that the president had been lying for years.

There was now no doubt that the full House would vote for impeachment and that there would be a trial in the Senate. That could drag on for months, but inevitably Nixon would be convicted and removed from office.

The Republican leadership, the president's top advisers, and even some members of his family believed that the best course was for Nixon to resign and spare himself and the country further turmoil. Still, a depressed and often disoriented Nixon waffled. One moment he indicated that he would resign. The next he said he would fight to the end.

On August 8, 1974, Nixon went on television to announce his resignation. The following day he sent a one-sentence letter of resignation to the Secretary of State and made an emotional farewell speech to the White House staff.

Then, accompanied by his wife, and his daughter Tricia and her husband, he boarded a waiting helicopter and left the White House forever.

Vice President Gerald Ford was sworn in as president. In his inaugural speech he announced "our long national nightmare is over."

AFTERMATH

After the resignation of Richard Nixon many of those who had worked for him still had to face trial for Watergate-related offenses. The five men originally arrested in the Watergate served from four to fifteen months in prison. Haldeman and Erlichman each served eighteen months; John Mitchell got nineteen months. Howard Hunt served thirty-three months in jail; and Gordon Liddy, who refused to the end to talk, served the most time in jail, fifty-two months.

Many others, like John Dean and Charles Colson, pleaded guilty to lesser charges and got reduced sentences.

On September 8, 1974, President Gerald Ford granted Nixon a full pardon for "all offenses against the United States which he, Richard Nixon, has committed or may have committed." Ford said that when Nixon accepted the pardon it was tantamount to an admission of guilt.

Ford insisted that there had never been a deal that a pardon would be granted in return for resignation. He said the only reason for the pardon was to spare the nation further agony. The move, however, was an unpopular one and may well have cost Ford the election when he ran for president in his own right in 1976.

Richard Nixon spent the rest of his life (he died in 1994) trying to reestablish his own reputation. He wrote several books and often spoke out on political affairs, particularly foreign policy.

Though he regained a measure of respectability, he was never forgiven. Part of the reason was that virtually everyone involved in Watergate wrote his own recollections of what happened and added more details—often unflattering ones—to the story. And then there were the tapes. Hundreds of hours of tapes were not made public during Watergate. Nixon fought tenaciously to keep them from ever being heard. But bit by bit they have been coming out, and much of the information has been damaging to Nixon's reputation. Whatever else Richard Nixon may have accomplished in his life, his political epitaph will always be Watergate.

Watergate was a tragic event in American history. Its worst effect was that it left the public more suspicious and cynical than ever about its political leadership. Every potential scandal is now dubbed "gate"—Irangate, Whitewatergate, Travelgate, and so on.

The best news to come out of Watergate was that a traumatic transition of power in the most powerful nation on earth was accomplished smoothly and without violence. Most of the nation watched events play out on television, and then went about their daily business. There were no riots, no barricades in the streets, no troops surrounding the White House.

The system worked as it was designed to—but just barely.

WANTED

| JAMES McCORD | DWIGHT CHAPIN | H. R. HALDEMAN | JOHN MITCHELL | JOHN ERLICHMAN |

| MAURICE STANS | EUGENIO MARTINEZ | G. GORDON LIDDY | CHARLES COLSON | HERBERT KALMBACH |

| JOHN DEAN | ROBERT MARDIAN | JEB MAGRUDER | RICHARD M. NIXON | BERNARD L. BARKER |

| VIRGILIO GONZALEZ | DONALD SEGRETTI | FRANK A. STURGIS | E. HOWARD HUNT JR. | HUGH SLOAN JR. |

CHRONOLOGY

1968 November 5: Richard M. Nixon and Spiro Agnew elected president and vice president.

1970 July: Nixon approves plans for expanding domestic intelligence-gathering activities.

1971 June 13: *The New York Times* begins publication of the Pentagon Papers.

September 3–4: White House "Plumbers" Howard Hunt and Gordon Liddy organize break-in at the office of Daniel Ellsberg's psychiatrist.

1972 June 17: Five men arrested in the offices of the Democratic National Committee in the Watergate.

June 20: Nixon and chief-of-staff H. R. Haldeman discuss Watergate. The tape of this conversation contains a mysterious eighteen-minute gap.

June 23: Nixon and Haldeman discuss plan to derail FBI investigation of Watergate. The "smoking gun" tape.

September 15: Hunt, Liddy, and five Watergate burglars indicted on federal charges.

November 7: Nixon/Agnew ticket reelected in a landslide.

1973 January 8–30: Trial of seven men indicted in Watergate burglary. All either plead guilty or are found guilty.

February 7: Senate establishes a select committee to investigate Watergate. Senator Sam Ervin named as chairman.

March 23: Judge John Sirica reads letter from Watergate burglar James McCord in open court. McCord charges there is a cover-up.

April 30: Nixon announces the resignations of Haldeman, John Erlichman, and Richard Kleindienst and the dismissal of John Dean.

May 17: Ervin Committee begins televised hearings.

May 18: Archibald Cox named Special Prosecutor.

June 25–29: Dean testifies before Ervin Committee, implicates President Nixon.

July 13: Alexander Butterfield reveals the existence of a White House taping system.

July 25: Nixon cites executive privilege in refusing to turn over subpoenaed tapes.

October 10: Vice President Agnew resigns.

October 20: The Saturday Night Massacre. Cox is fired, attorney general and deputy attorney general resign.

November 1: Leon Jaworski named new special prosecutor.

1974 April 20: Nixon announces release of edited transcripts of tapes.

July 24: Supreme Court rules 8-0 that the president must turn over tapes.

Televised hearings on impeachment by House Judiciary Committee begin.

July 27–30: House committee votes to recommend three articles of impeachment.

August 5: White House releases full transcript of "smoking gun" tape.

August 8: Nixon's televised announcement of resignation.

August 9: President Nixon resigns; Gerald Ford becomes president.

September 8: Ford grants Nixon full pardon for involvement in Watergate.

FURTHER READING

Cook, Fred J. *The Crimes of Watergate*. New York: Franklin Watts, 1981.

Hargrove, Jim. *The Story of Watergate*. Chicago: The Children's Press, 1988.

Herda, D. J. *United States v. Nixon: Watergate and the President*. Springfield N.J.: Enslow, 1996.

Morin, Isobel. *Impeaching the President*. Brookfield, CT.: Millbrook Press, 1996.

BIBLIOGRAPHY

Bernstein, Carl, and Bob Woodward. *All the President's Men.* New York: Simon & Schuster, 1974.

Dean, John W. III. *Blind Ambition: The White House Years.* New York: Simon & Schuster, 1976.

Emery, Fred. *Watergate.* New York: Times Books, 1994.

Ervin, Sam J., Jr. *The Whole Truth.* New York: Random House, 1980.

Liddy, G. Gordon. *Will.* New York: St. Martin's, 1980.

Lukas, J. Anthony. *Nightmare: The Underside of the Nixon Years.* New York: Viking, 1976.

Nixon, Richard M., *RN: The Memoirs of Richard Nixon.* New York: Grosset & Dunlap, 1975.

Staff of *The Washington Post. The Presidential Transcripts.* New York: Dell, 1974.

White, Theodore H. *Breach of Faith: The Fall of Richard Nixon.* New York: Atheneum, 1973.

Woodward, Bob, and Carl Bernstein. *The Final Days.* New York: Simon & Schuster, 1976.

INDEX

Democratic National Convention (1968), 19

Douglas, Helen Gahagan, 16, *17*

Ehrlichman, John, 25, 37, 39, 40, 53

Eisenhower, Dwight D., 16, *17*, 18

Ellsberg, Daniel, 23, 27, 30

Ervin, Sam, 37, 40

Ervin Committee, 37, 38, 40, 42, 50

Federal Bureau of Investigation (FBI), 20, 24, 31, 37, 40

Fielding, Lewis, 27, 28

Ford, Gerald, 32, 52, 54

Gray, L. Patrick, 31, 34, 40

Haig, Alexander, 43

Haldeman, H.R. "Bob," 26, 39, 40, 45, 52, 53

Hoover, J. Edgar, 24, *25*, 31

House Judiciary Committee, 48, 50

Humphrey, Hubert, 19

Hunt, Dorothy, 37

Hunt, E. Howard, Jr., 13, *26*, 26-28, 30, 31, 37, 40, 53

Impeachment proceedings, 48-50, 52

Jackson State University, 23

Jaworski, Leon, 43, 48

Johnson, Andrew, 49

Johnson, Lyndon, 19

Justice, Department of, 37, 43

Kennedy, Edward M., 26

Kennedy, John F., 18, 26, 27

Kent State University, 22, *22*

Kleindienst, Richard, 31, 39, 42

Leeper, Paul, 8

Liddy, G. Gordon, *26*, 26-28, 30, 31, 33, 53

Magruder, Jeb, 30

McCord, James, 11, 13, 28, 31, 34, 36-37

McGovern, George, 13, 14, 29

Mitchell, John, 25, 38-40, 50

New York Times, The, 23, *39*

Nixon, Pat, 52